Leatherback Turtle Migration

by Grace Hansen

Abdo
ANIMAL MIGRATION
Kids

abdopublishing.com

Published by Abdo Kids, a division of ABDO, P.O. Box 398166, Minneapolis, Minnesota 55439.

Printed in the United States of America, North Mankato, Minnesota.

052017

092017

 THIS BOOK CONTAINS
RECYCLED MATERIALS

Photo Credits: Alamy, Glow Images, iStock, Minden Pictures, National Geographic Creative,
Science Source, Shutterstock

Production Contributors: Teddy Borth, Jennie Forsberg, Grace Hansen

Design Contributors: Dorothy Toth, Laura Mitchell

Publisher's Cataloging in Publication Data

Names: Hansen, Grace, author.

Title: Leatherback turtle migration / by Grace Hansen.

Description: Minneapolis, Minnesota : Abdo Kids, 2018 | Series: Animal migration
    | Includes bibliographical references and index.

Identifiers: LCCN 2016962366 | ISBN 9781532100291 (lib. bdg.) |
    ISBN 9781532100987 (ebook) | ISBN 9781532101533 (Read-to-me ebook)

Subjects: LCSH: Leatherback turtle--Juvenile literature. | Leatherback turtle
    migration--Juvenile literature.

Classification: DDC 597.92--dc23

LC record available at http://lccn.loc.gov/2016962366

Table of Contents

Leatherback Turtles

Leatherback turtles live in seas and oceans around the world. They can be found as far north as Alaska. Some have been spotted near southern Africa.

4

Leatherbacks are the largest turtles in the world. They can grow up to 10 feet (3m) long. They can weigh up to 2,000 pounds (907 kg).

Leatherbacks travel more
than any other sea turtle.
Some leatherbacks swim as far
as 10,000 miles (16,093 km)
each year!

9

Leatherbacks spend most of their time in cold water far from the **equator**. They feed on jellyfish and other soft-bodied **invertebrates**.

Once females have eaten plenty, they will **mate**. Then begins their great journey.

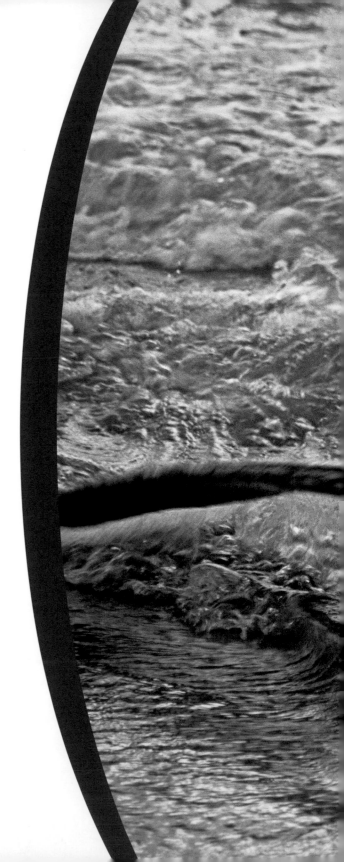

The Long Swim

Females will swim to **tropical** beaches near the **equator**. This is where they lay their eggs.

14

Most female leatherbacks will return to the same beach each year. Others will choose different beaches in the same area.

17

The female finds a safe place to lay her eggs. She digs and lays her eggs in a hole. She then covers the eggs with sand.